Little ECO EXPERTS

Let's Learn About the Biosphere

**Translated by
Diana Osorio**

**How to be
guardians of
the planet**

PowerKiDS press.

Published in 2023 by PowerKids, an Imprint of Rosen Publishing
29 East 21st Street, New York, NY 10010

Cataloging-in-Publication Data
Names: Editorial Sol 90 (Firm).
Title: Let's learn about the biosphere / by the editors at Sol90.
Description: New York : Powerkids Press, 2023. | Series: Little eco experts
| Includes glossary and index.
Identifiers: ISBN 9781725337206 (pbk.) | ISBN 9781725337220 (library
bound) | ISBN 9781725337213 (6pack) | ISBN 9781725337237 (ebook)
Subjects: LCSH: Biosphere--Juvenile literature.
Classification: LCC QH343.4 L48 2023 | DDC 333.95--dc23

Coordination: Nuria Cicero
Editor: Alberto Hernández
Editor, Spanish: Diana Osorio
Layout: Àngels Rambla
Design Adaptation: Raúl Rodriguez, R studio T, NYC
Project Team: Vicente Ponce, Rosa Salvía, Paola Fornasaro
Scientific Advisory Services: Teresa Martínez Barchino

Imaging and Infographics:
www.infographics90.com
Firms: Getty/Thinkstock, AGE Fotostock, Cordon Press/Corbis,
Shutterstock.

Manufactured in the United States of America

CPSIA Compliance Information: Batch #CSPK23. For Further Information
contact Rosen Publishing, New York, New York at 1-800-237-9932.

Find us on

CONTENTS

WHAT IS THE BIOSPHERE?

The biosphere is the land, sea, and air on our planet where life is possible. It is the space where living creatures are found, from insects, plants, and other smaller organisms to human beings.

From the Surface to the Core

From far above the surface of Earth to its center, only a few miles can harbor life. In this small area, life depends on energy from the sun and the circulation of heat and essential nutrients.

The Air

The atmosphere is a layer of gases stretching up from the planet's surface about 6,200 miles (10,000 km). It's a huge protective shield for Earth. Of those thousands of miles, only a few are suitable for the development of life.

DID YOU KNOW?

Some living organisms can survive several miles beneath the surface of the ocean.

SO MANY SPECIES

Plants and Trees

All plants are living beings, including trees. Many are homes for other kinds of organisms, including small parasites like some kinds of fungi and birds that nest in trees.

Animal Life

As of today, over 1.2 million species of animals have been identified. And scientists believe that, in reality, there are about 8.7 million in total.

Biodiversity is the variety of all forms of life throughout terrestrial and marine ecosystems on the planet.

Marine Life

Oceans and rivers are inhabited by countless species: algae, lichen, corals, reptiles, fish, mammals, insects, and many, many more.

ANIMALS BY GROUPS

Mammals

Mammals are, perhaps, the most well-known animals, but the least numerous. There are about 6,500 different species of mammals, and they are monophyletic, which means they descend from a common ancestor.

Birds

There are a great variety. Many fly through the skies, others can't fly at all, and yet others know how to swim. The more than 10,000 species are found on all continents.

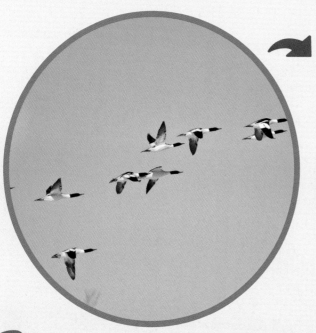

Reptiles and Amphibians

Terrestrial or aquatic, or both, reptiles and amphibians inhabit many kinds of ecosystems. They add up to more than 16,000 species.

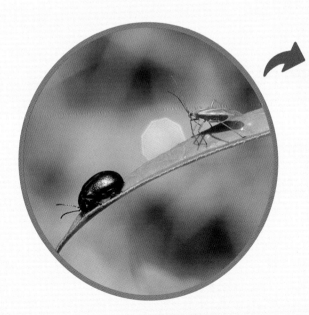

Invertebrates

Invertebrates—insects, mollusks, spiders, worms, and more—are found all over and represent 95 percent of the animals on Earth.

THE LOSS OF BIODIVERSITY

When the human population increases, there is a growing need for space to construct homes, offices, and more buildings. And as construction grows, biodiversity disappears.

Wild Areas

Forests, savannas, swamps, and deserts are under threat. Every organism that lives in these places is at risk.

Deforestation

By opening up space for homes or crops in forests and not replanting, the animal populations suffer greatly.

After

Animals

By changing the course of a river or modifying another natural path, animals can lose their food sources and mating sites.

Building

When large irrigation systems or hydroelectric dams are built, the course of rivers may be modified, forests can become flooded, and species can disappear.

NATURAL PARADISES

Cap de Creus

At the easternmost point of the Iberian peninsula, in Catalonia, is the Cap de Creus, a wild coastal landscape spotted with small islands, steep cliffs, and hidden coves. It is a biological paradise with rock formations sculpted by water erosion, green forests, and a rich marine life.

With 375,000 square miles (972,000 sq km), Northeast Greenland National Park is the largest in the world. It was created to protect the delicate flora and fauna of the island.

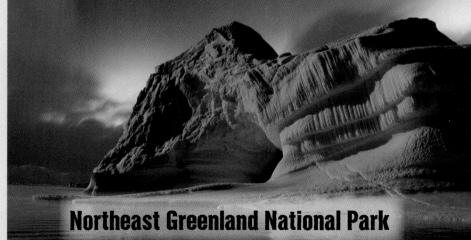

Northeast Greenland National Park

Natural spaces are areas of Earth that have not been modified by humans. This term includes natural and national parks, protected areas, and virgin forests.

Centla Swamps

The Pantanos de Centla (Centla Swamps) in Mexico were declared a Biosphere Reserve by UNESCO to guarantee the preservation of the living organisms that reside there. In this area, varied ecosystems with differentiated flora and fauna coexist.

Christmas Island

More than half of Christmas Island, to the west of Australia, is a protected national park. Its isolation and minimum human intervention have encouraged the development of its unique flora and fauna. It is of great interest to scientists.

A UNIQUE ECOSYSTEM

Of Global Interest

Consisting of 3,040 square miles (7,880 sq km) of islands of volcanic origin, the Galápagos Islands are under special protection by Ecuador and the international community.

Giant Turtles

Sea and Shore Birds

The Galápagos Islands are located in the Pacific Ocean, about 560 miles (900 km) off the coast of Ecuador, where large ocean currents converge. This archipelago is a unique maritime and terrestrial habitat due to its wide biodiversity.

51,000 square miles (132,000 sq km)

is the area of the Galápagos Marine Reserve, a World Heritage Site.

Thanks to Darwin

Does the name Charles Darwin ring a bell? He is the famous British naturalist who investigated the evolution of species. He visited the Galápagos in 1835 and was the first who described many species that lived there.

Diverse Wildlife

IN DANGER
OF EXTINCTION

Red Panda

Eastern Tuna

South China Tiger

Baiji

Giant Panda

Hyacinth Macaw

Risk Classification

Extinct in Its Habitat ●

A species that now only survives under human protection.

Critical Risk ●

The demise of the species is imminent and almost unavoidable.

It might be due to human intervention or natural causes, but the reality is thousands of species could disappear from the face of the planet. Look these cases:

Cross River Gorilla   **Hawksbill Sea Turtle**   **Black Rhinoceros**

Santa Cruz Giant Tortoise   **Panamanian Golden Toad**   **Lynx**

At Risk ●

The population of the species is declining quickly.

Vulnerable ○

There is a high risk that this species will begin to disappear.

MAMMALS IN DANGER

Almost one in four mammals are at risk of total disappearance due to the destruction of their habitats. Pollution, deforestation, and poaching are their biggest threats.

African Giants

Some large animals such as the rhinoceros, the elephant, and the hippopotamus are also at great risk. These animals can weigh more than a ton and are herbivores.

There are several species of rhinoceros that are in danger of extinction. The main cause is illegal hunting and changes in their habitat.

Black Rhinoceros

Orangutan

Primates

This order is the most affected among all mammals. Almost half of this species is at risk because of the destruction of forests and illegal specimen trade.

The orangutan is at risk of extinction. Its habitat is in Indonesia and Malaysia, where various organizations are devoted to saving the species.

Cetaceans

This is another group of mammals at great risk, especially smaller coastal and freshwater species.

The blue whale, considered the biggest animal on Earth, was illegally hunted for a long time.

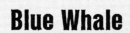

Blue Whale

AMPHIBIANS AT RISK

Veragua Stubfoot Toad

This species is critically endangered. It is captured for illegal trade because of its colors. Deforestation has destroyed much of its habitat in Costa Rica as well.

Golden Toad

It is not yet known what has been the cause for the disappearance of this species. Perhaps it was due to acid rain or small changes in the environment around it.

According to the International Union for the Conservation of Nature, amphibian populations around the world are declining faster than other groups of animals. More than 30 percent of species are listed as threatened.

Spotted Salamander

Its habitat is in the forest, so urban growth and deforestation directly threaten it, as does environmental pollution.

Argentine Horned Frog

It is critically endangered because its population has dropped about 80 percent in the past decades. This decline has been attributed to a fungus that poisons anphibians.

HOW ILLEGAL HUNTING IS DANGEROUS

There is legal and illegal hunting. The former is regulated and authorizes hunting of animals when populations have increased. But if hunting is illegal, it can lead to the extinction of species.

Fugitive Poachers

Poachers kill to exhibit the skins or heads of the animals they hunt as trophies. Many people see it as a sport, but it should not considered as such.

Fur Rugs

Head Trophies

Many countries have banned the importing of hunting trophies.

The Ivory Business

The populations of African and Asian elephants have decreased alarmingly due to the value of the ivory in their tusks.

Objects Made of Ivory

Medicinal Use

The tiger population in Asia is almost nonexistent as this big cat is often hunted. What is the reason? Tiger parts are used for traditional Chinese medicine, which has not been proven to be effective.

Hunted animals, even those who aren't killed, endure fear and stress.

In Fashion

Entire populations of birds, lizards, and reptiles have been decimated for the use of their feathers and skins in articles of clothing.

Many organizations are working to end the international trade of animal skin.

In the Ocean

Shark fishing is punishable by law in many parts of the world. There are people who believe that the fins of sharks have medicinal properties. And these are not the only marine species that are in danger due to illegal fishing.

A Complex Issue

Farmers and ranchers often set traps to defend their farms against animals that can be harmful to them, such as foxes. In other cases, humans may kill animals that are not even harming them, such as whales.

In Decoration

Not only are mammalian species hunted to later be objects of decoration and exhibition, but also fish, birds, and reptiles.

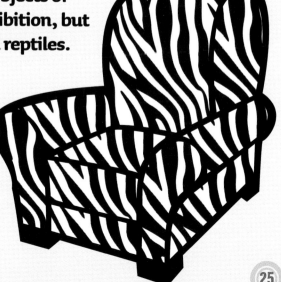

Thanks to technological advances, fabrics can be created to imitate the skin of almost every animal. Always choose to buy synthetic as opposed to natural skins.

Choose Synthetic Fabrics

THE SEA SUFFERS

Uncontrolled fishing endangers both marine species and the very balance of ecosystems. That is why responsible conservation measures are in place in many areas of the world.

Responsible Fishing

This means meeting certain requirements and knowing what species to fish. It does not involve the use of toxic or dangerous products, and it does not discard any living thing caught; everything is used.

Young Fishes

If selected young fish are overfished, they cannot become adults to reproduce. That puts the future of species in danger.

Coral Reefs

Uncontrolled fishing affects the necessary balance for the health of reefs, important marine habitats due to their biodiversity.

WHAT IS TRAWLING?

Trawling is very efficient, but it is not ecological at all. It is done with a net that is used to "sweep" the seabed, capturing everything it finds. It is not selective, and it destroys the ecosystem.

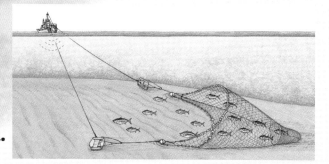

THE ADVANCE OF DESERTS

Since prehistoric times, deserts have expanded and decreased according to environmental conditions. But with humankind's spread, arid and unusable lands have multiplied. Let's see how it happens:

Once nutrients have been depleted, the soil loses its fertility and is abandoned.

The vegetation cover is removed to use the soil for agricultural production.

Degradation Process

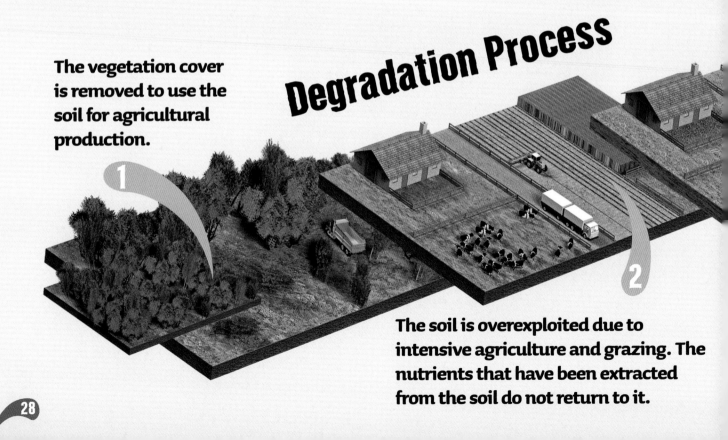

The soil is overexploited due to intensive agriculture and grazing. The nutrients that have been extracted from the soil do not return to it.

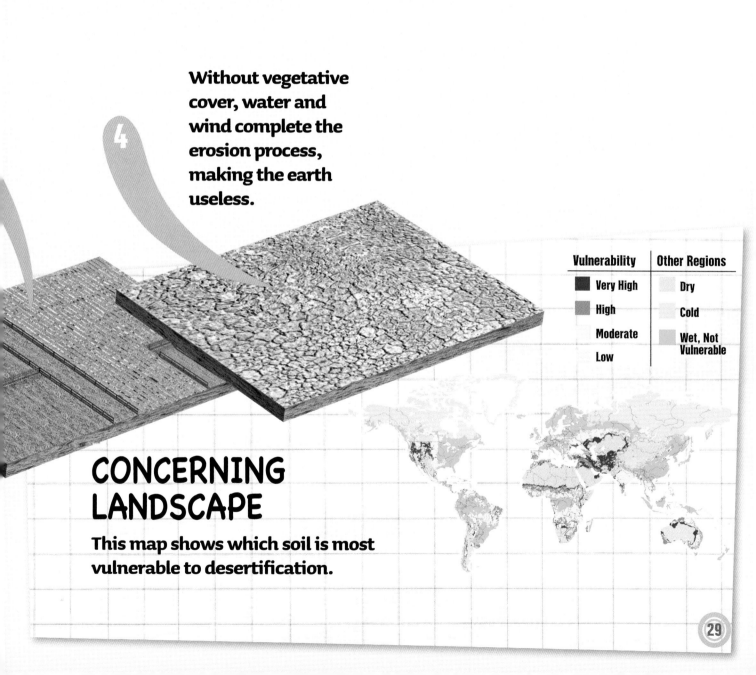

Without vegetative cover, water and wind complete the erosion process, making the earth useless.

4

Vulnerability	Other Regions
■ Very High	Dry
High	Cold
Moderate	Wet, Not Vulnerable
Low	

CONCERNING LANDSCAPE

This map shows which soil is most vulnerable to desertification.

THE ECOLOGICAL FOOTPRINT

For decades, the ecological footprint has been the most accepted indicator to measure the impact of humans on the planet.

Measurement

It is a calculation of the ecologically productive area that a country or region consumes to generate the resources it uses and to deal with the waste it produces.

Farmlands

Rangelands

Forests

Carbon Absorption

Urbanized Lands

Fishing Areas

How Is It Measured?

An estimate is made using data relating to six areas based on the type of surface: crops, pastures, forests, urbanized land, fishing areas, and carbon absorption areas.

Why Is It Important?

Without realizing it in our daily life, we perform many activities that have an impact on our habitat. And the environment must deal with that impact. That is why the ecological footprint is so important, because nature is not indestructible. It can be damaged.

WHAT CAN YOU DO?

Biodiversity is a huge treasure that you own. Protect it and be an eco-expert following these 5 SUGGESTIONS:

1 A problem that threatens biodiversity is the traffic of exotic species. Many do not tolerate the travel or die soon after being removed from their natural habitat. Don't buy exotic animals.

2 Avoid buying products like furs, feathers, or eggs that come from endangered species.

3 If you buy a pet, make sure it is not an endangered species. It is better to choose a native species.

4 Try not to buy exotic plants. There is a risk that they cannot adapt to a new home.

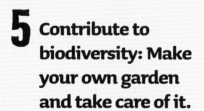

5 Contribute to biodiversity: Make your own garden and take care of it.

NATURAL FLEA SPRAY

Chemical pesticides are big pollutants. Help the environment by using this safe and natural mixture to keep fleas away from your pets.

YOU WILL NEED:
- Orange peel
- 1 cup of water
- Blender
- Pot
- Cotton
- Plastic or glass container

STEP BY STEP: Find the instructions on the next page!

STEP ONE

Cut the orange peel into small pieces and grind it with the help of a blender.

STEP TWO

Add 1 cup of water to the blender and blend it again.

STEP THREE

Pour the mixture into a pot and boil it, with the help of an adult. Then, lower the temperature. Simmer 5 minutes.

STEP FOUR

Let it cool off, and pour the mixture into a plastic or glass container. You can now rub this mixture onto your pet's skin using a cotton ball or pad.

Conclusion

Fleas hate acids, such as vinegar or citrus; that's why this smell drives them away. This is a healthy and natural option to repel fleas and take care of our pets.

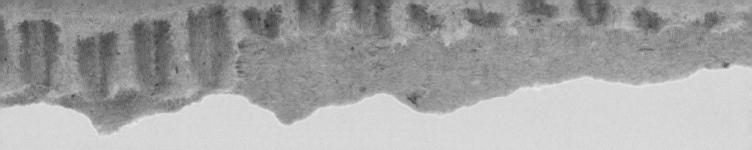

Glossary

archipelago: a group of islands

cetacean: a kind of marine mammal, such as a dolphin or whale

deplete: to lessen

ecological: having to do with how living organisms relate to one another and to their surroundings

exotic: coming from a distant country

fauna: animals in an area

flora: plants in an area

irrigation: the watering of a dry area by man-made means to grow plants

nutrient: something a living thing needs to grow and stay alive

parasite: a living thing that lives in, on, or with another living thing and harms it

pesticide: something used to kill pests, such as bugs

poaching: illegally killing or capturing wild animals

Index